# Thoughts from the pen of a Pope

## Pope Benedict XVI

### 16 April 1927 - 31 December 2022

GW00683791

redemptorist
publications

Published by Redemptorist Publications
Wolf's Lane, Chawton, Hampshire, GU34 3HQ, UK
Tel. +44 (0)1420 88222, Fax. +44 (0)1420 88805
Email rp@rpbooks.co.uk, www.rpbooks.co.uk

A registered charity limited by guarantee
Registered in England 03261721

Copyright © Redemptorist Publications 2023

Edited by Sr Janet Fearns FMDM
Designed by Eliana Thompson

ISBN 978-0-85231-560-6

A CIP catalogue record for this book is available
from the British Library

The publisher gratefully acknowledges permission
to use the following copyright material:

Excerpts from the English translation and chants
of The Roman Missal

Quotes are taken from the official Vatican website:
http://w2.vatican.va/content/benedict-xvi/en.html

Cover quote: Concelebrated Mass with the members
of the International Theological Commission

Cover photograph of Pope Benedict XVI © Mazur/
catholicnews.org.uk

Every effort has been made to trace copyright holders
and to obtain their permission for the use of copyright
material. The publisher apologises for any errors or
omissions and would be grateful for notification of
any corrections that should be incorporated in future
reprints or editions of this book.

Printed by Lithgo Press Ltd., Leicester LE8 6NU

# Contents

1

# The small child

Tittmoning remains my childhood land of dreams...
Above all, the shop windows illuminated at night
during the Christmas season have remained in
my memory like a wonderful promise... We liked
to cross over to nearby Austria. There was a special
feeling in "going to a foreign country" by just
taking a few steps... I also remember the attic
where a friend would stage his puppet theatre
for us, with figures that fired our imagination...

Father thus decided, toward the end of 1932,
to change locations once more. In Tittmoning
he had simply said too much against the
brownshirts. In December, shortly before
Christmas, we moved into our new home in
Aschau am Inn... We were assigned the second
storey and there we found all the makings of a
cosy home.

A front garden with a lovely wayside cross
belonged to the house, and also a big meadow
with a carp pond in which I almost drowned
once while playing.

Joseph Ratzinger, *Milestones: Memoirs*, 1927-1977
(San Francisco: Ignatius Press, 1998), 10

# Traunstein

Over the years our mother created a splendid home from the slightly dilapidated house that Father had fixed up... The structural condition of this house caused Father all kinds of trouble, but for us children it was a paradise beyond our wildest dreams...

With our move to Traunstein [1933], however, new and serious concerns entered my life. A few days after our arrival the school opened its doors. I now entered the first class... I was the youngest and one of the smallest in the whole class...

Early in 1938 no one could ignore the movement of troops. There was talk of war against Austria, until one day we heard that the German army had marched into that country...

About this time a quite radical change occurred in my life. For two years I had been very happily going from home to school every day, but now the pastor urged me to enter the minor seminary... For my father, whose pension was very scant indeed, this represented a great sacrifice.

Ratzinger: *Milestones*, 22

## 3

# Minor seminary

I am one of those people who are not made for living in a boarding school... Now I had to sit in a study hall with about sixty other boys, and this was such a torture to me that studying, which had always come so easily to me, now appeared almost impossible... I am not at all gifted at sports and also because I was the youngest of all the boys, some of whom were as much as three years older than I. Thus, I was inferior to most in physical strength...

Meanwhile the drama of history was becoming increasingly grave with every violent act of the Third Reich... At first the war appeared to be almost unreal... Alongside this experience, however, there also stood the fact that almost every day the newspaper informed us of some soldier's death, and almost every day a requiem Mass had to be held for a young man.

Ratzinger: *Milestones*, 25

# Ordination

We were more than forty candidates, who, at
the solemn call on that radiant summer day,
which I remember as the high point of my life,
responded "*Adsum*", Here I am. We should not
be superstitious; but, at that moment when the
elderly archbishop laid his hands on me, a little
bird – perhaps a lark – flew up from the high altar
in the cathedral and trilled a little joyful song.
And I could not but see in this a reassurance from
on high, as if I heard the words "This is good, you
are on the right way."…

On the day of our first Holy Mass, our parish
church of Saint Oswald gleamed in all its
splendour, and the joy that almost palpably
filled the whole place drew everyone there into
the most living mode of active participation.

We were invited to bring the first blessing into
people's homes, and everywhere we were received
even by total strangers with a warmth and
affection I had not thought possible until that day.

Ratzinger: *Milestones*, 99

# A new pope

One of the basic characteristics of a shepherd must be to love the people entrusted to him, even as he loves Christ whom he serves. "Feed my sheep", says Christ to Peter, and now, at this moment, he says it to me as well. Feeding means loving, and loving also means being ready to suffer. Loving means giving the sheep what is truly good, the nourishment of God's truth, of God's word, the nourishment of his presence, which he gives us in the Blessed Sacrament. My dear friends – at this moment I can only say: pray for me, that I may learn to love the Lord more and more. Pray for me, that I may learn to love his flock more and more – in other words, you, the holy Church, each one of you and all of you together. Pray for me, that I may not flee for fear of the wolves. Let us pray for one another, that the Lord will carry us and that we will learn to carry one another.

Inauguration Mass,
24 April 2005

The unfolding story

# Sixty years a priest

"I no longer call you servants, but friends."

Sixty years on from the day of my priestly ordination, I hear once again deep within me these words of Jesus that were addressed to us new priests at the end of the ordination ceremony by the Archbishop, Cardinal Faulhaber, in his slightly frail yet firm voice. According to the liturgical practice of that time, these words conferred on the newly-ordained priests the authority to forgive sins. "No longer servants, but friends": at that moment I knew deep down that these words were no mere formality, nor were they simply a quotation from Scripture. I knew that, at that moment, the Lord himself was speaking to me in a very personal way... "You are no longer servants, but friends": these words bring great inner joy, but at the same time, they are so awe-inspiring that one can feel daunted as the decades go by amid so many experiences of one's own frailty and his inexhaustible goodness.

Mass for the imposition of the pallium
on metropolitan archbishops, 29 June 2011

# Love in God and with God

In God and with God, I love even the person whom I do not like or even know... I learn to look on this other person not simply with my eyes and my feelings, but from the perspective of Jesus Christ. His friend is my friend. Going beyond exterior appearances, I perceive in others an interior desire for a sign of love, of concern... Seeing with the eyes of Christ, I can give to others much more than their outward necessities; I can give them the look of love which they crave... Only my readiness to encounter my neighbour and to show him love makes me sensitive to God as well. Only if I serve my neighbour can my eyes be opened to what God does for me and how much he loves me.

Pope Benedict XVI, *Deus Caritas Est*, ("God is Love"), 18

# Christian love

For love... as the content of being a Christian, demands that we try to live and God lives. He loves us, not because we are especially good, particularly virtuous, or of any great merit, not because we are useful or even necessary to him; he loves us, not because *we* are good, but because *he* is good. He loves us, although we have nothing to offer him; he loves us even in the ragged raiment of the prodigal son, who is no longer wearing anything lovable. To love in the Christian sense means trying to follow in this path; not just loving someone we like, who pleases us, who suits us, and certainly not just someone who has something to offer us or from whom we are hoping to gain some advantage.

Practising Christian love in the same way as Christ means that we are good to someone who needs our kindness, even if we do not like him.

Joseph Ratzinger, *Credo for Today: What Christians Believe*, (San Francisco: Ignatius Press, 2009), 10

# Christian and Catholic

What is the most fascinating thing about being Catholic for you personally?

The fascinating thing is this great living history into which we enter. Looked at in purely human terms, it is something extraordinary. That an institution with so many human weaknesses and failures is nonetheless preserved in its continuity and that I, living within this great communion, can know that I am in communion with all the living and the dead; and that I also find in it a certainty about the essence of my life – namely God who has turned to me – on which I can found my life, with which I can live and die.

Peter Seewald and Joseph Ratzinger,
*Salt of the Earth: An Exclusive Interview on the State of the Church at the End of the Millennium*,
(San Francisco: Ignatius Press, 1997), 20

# The invisible but powerful Lord

No, we cannot see [Jesus in the Eucharist], but
there are many things that we do not see but they
exist and are essential. For example: we do not
see our reason, yet we have reason. We do not see
our intelligence and we have it. In a word: we do
not see our soul and yet it exists and we see its
effects, because we can speak, think and make
decisions... Therefore, we do not see the very
deepest things, those that really sustain life and
the world, but we can see and feel their effects.

So it is with the Risen Lord: we do not see him
with our eyes but we see that wherever Jesus is,
people change, they improve. A greater capacity
for peace, for reconciliation, etc., is created.
Therefore, we do not see the Lord himself but we
see the effects of the Lord: so we can understand
that Jesus is present.

Catechetical meeting with children who had
received their First Communion during the year,
15 October 2005

# Jesus brought us God

What has Jesus really brought, then, if he has not brought world peace, universal prosperity, and a better world? What has he brought? The answer is very simple: God. He has brought God! He has brought the God who once gradually unveiled his countenance first to Abraham, then to Moses and the prophets, and then in the wisdom literature – the God who showed his face only in Israel, even though he was also honoured among the pagans in various shadowy guises. It is this God, the God of Abraham, of Isaac, and of Jacob, the true God, whom he has brought to the peoples of the earth. He has brought God, and now we know his face, now we can call upon him. Now we know the path that we human beings have to take in this world. Jesus has brought God and with God the truth about where we are going and where we come from: faith, hope, and love.

Joseph Ratzinger, *Jesus of Nazareth: From the Baptism in the Jordan to the Transfiguration*, (London: Bloomsbury, 2008), 44

# The "power" of Jesus

In what does this "power" of Jesus Christ the King consist? It is not the power of the kings or the great people of this world; it is the divine power to give eternal life, to liberate from evil, to defeat the dominion of death. It is the power of Love that can draw good from evil, that can melt a hardened heart, bring peace amid the harshest conflict and kindle hope in the thickest darkness. This Kingdom of Grace is never imposed and always respects our freedom. Christ came "to bear witness to the truth", as he declared to Pilate: whoever accepts his witness serves beneath his "banner", according to the image dear to St Ignatius of Loyola. Every conscience, therefore, must make a choice. Who do I want to follow? God or the Evil One? The truth or falsehood? Choosing Christ does not guarantee success according to the world's criteria but assures the peace and joy that he alone can give us.

Angelus,
22 November 2009

# The soul of the Church

What is this "power" of the Holy Spirit? It is the power of God's life! It is the power of the same Spirit who hovered over the waters at the dawn of creation and who, in the fullness of time, raised Jesus from the dead. It is the power which points us, and our world, towards the coming of the Kingdom of God. In today's Gospel, Jesus proclaims that a new age has begun, in which the Holy Spirit will be poured out upon all humanity. He himself, conceived by the Holy Spirit and born of the Virgin Mary, came among us to bring us that Spirit. As the source of our new life in Christ, the Holy Spirit is also, in a very real way, the soul of the Church, the love which binds us to the Lord and one another, and the light which opens our eyes to see all around us the wonders of God's grace.

Celebration of vespers with bishops, priests, men and
women religious, ecclesial and pastoral movements of Galilee,
20 July 2008

The Holy Spirit

# The Holy Spirit is joy

An integral part of any celebration is joy. A celebration can be organized, joy cannot. It can only be offered as a gift; and in fact it has been given to us in abundance. For this we are grateful. Just as Paul describes joy as a fruit of the Holy Spirit, so John in his Gospel closely links the Spirit to joy. The Holy Spirit gives us joy. And he is joy. Joy is the gift that sums up all the other gifts. It is the expression of happiness, of being in harmony with ourselves, which can only come from being in harmony with God and with his creation.

It is part of the nature of joy to spread, to be shared. The Church's missionary spirit is nothing other than the drive to share the joy that has been given to us. May that joy always be alive in us, and thus shine forth upon our troubled world.

Address to the Roman Curia for the traditional
exchange of Christmas greetings,
22 December 2008

# True Mother of God

Mary, in fact, is the true Mother of God precisely by virtue of her total relationship to Christ. Therefore, in glorifying the Son one honours the Mother and in honouring the Mother one glorifies the Son... Indeed, Mary did not receive God's gift for herself alone, but in order to bring him into the world: in her fruitful virginity, God gave men and women the gifts of eternal salvation. And Mary continually offers her mediation to the People of God, on pilgrimage through history towards eternity, just as she once offered it to the shepherds of Bethlehem. She, who gave earthly life to the Son of God, continues to give human beings divine life, which is Jesus himself and his Holy Spirit. For this reason she is considered the Mother of every human being who is born to Grace and at the same time is invoked as Mother of the Church.

Mass for Solemnity of Mary, Mother of God
and 44th World Day of Peace,
1 January 2011

# Mary, our Mother

Mary, in whose virginal womb God was made man, is our Mother! Indeed, from the Cross before bringing his sacrifice to completion, Jesus gave her to us as our Mother and entrusted us to her as her children. This is a mystery of mercy and love, a gift that enriches the Church with fruitful spiritual motherhood... Does not our Heavenly Mother invite us to shun evil and to do good, following with docility the divine law engraved in every Christian's heart? Does not she, who preserved her hope even at the peak of her trial, ask us not to lose heart when suffering and death comes knocking at the door of our homes? Does she not ask us to look confidently to our future? Does not the Immaculate Virgin exhort us to be brothers and sisters to one another, all united by the commitment to build together a world that is more just, supportive and peaceful?

Act of veneration to the Immaculate at the Spanish Steps,
8 December 2007

# St Joseph

Having given up the idea of divorcing Mary secretly, Joseph took her to himself because he then saw God's work in her with his own eyes... Although he had felt distressed, Joseph "did as the Angel of the Lord commanded him", certain that he was doing the right thing. And in giving the name of "Jesus" to the Child who rules the entire universe, he placed himself among the throng of humble and faithful servants... In witnessing to Mary's virginity, to God's gratuitous action and in safeguarding the Messiah's earthly life St Joseph announces the miracle of the Lord. Therefore let us venerate the legal father of Jesus because the new man is outlined in him, who looks with trust and courage to the future. He does not follow his own plans but entrusts himself without reserve to the infinite mercy of the One who will fulfil the prophecies and open the time of salvation.

Angelus,
19 December 2010

# Ss Peter and Paul

Christian tradition has always considered St Peter and St Paul to be inseparable: indeed, together, they represent the whole Gospel of Christ. In Rome, their bond as brothers in the faith came to acquire a particular significance. Indeed, the Christian community of this City considered them a kind of counterbalance to the mythical Romulus and Remus, the two brothers held to be the founders of Rome. A further parallel comes to mind, still on the theme of brothers: whereas the first biblical pair of brothers demonstrate the effects of sin, as Cain kills Abel, yet Peter and Paul, much as they differ from one another in human terms and notwithstanding the conflicts that arose in their relationship, illustrate a new way of being brothers, lived according to the Gospel, an authentic way made possible by the grace of Christ's Gospel working within them.

Mass for the imposition of the pallium
on metropolitan archbishops,
29 June 2012

# The family and peace

In a healthy family life we experience some of the fundamental elements of peace: justice and love between brothers and sisters, the role of authority expressed by parents, loving concern for the members who are weaker because of youth, sickness or old age, mutual help in the necessities of life, readiness to accept others and, if necessary, to forgive them. For this reason, the family is *the first and indispensable teacher of peace*…

The family is the foundation of society for this reason too: *because it enables its members in decisive ways to experience peace*. It follows that the human community cannot do without the service provided by the family. Where can young people gradually learn to savour the genuine "taste" of peace better than in the original "nest" which nature prepares for them? *The language of the family is a language of peace*; we must always draw from it, lest we lose the "vocabulary" of peace.

Message for the World Day of Peace,
1 January 2008

Family

# The real needs of a child

Every child's birth brings something of this mystery with it! Parents who receive a child as a gift know this well and often speak of it in this way. We have all heard people say to a father and a mother: "this child is a gift, a miracle!" ... How important it is, therefore, that every child coming into the world be welcomed by the warmth of a family! External comforts do not matter: Jesus was born in a stable and had a manger as his first cradle, but the love of Mary and of Joseph made him feel the tenderness and beauty of being loved. Children need this: the love of their father and mother. It is this that gives them security and, as they grow, enables them to discover the meaning of life. The Holy Family of Nazareth went through many trials... Yet, trusting in divine Providence, they found their stability and guaranteed Jesus a serene childhood and a sound upbringing.

Angelus,
26 December 2010

# God's creative love

The created world, structured in an intelligent way by God, is entrusted to our responsibility and though we are able to analyse it and transform it, we cannot consider ourselves creation's absolute master. We are called, rather, to exercise responsible stewardship of creation, in order to protect it, to enjoy its fruits, and to cultivate it, finding the resources necessary for everyone to live with dignity. Through the help of nature itself and through hard work and creativity, humanity is indeed capable of carrying out its grave duty to hand on the earth to future generations so that they too, in turn, will be able to inhabit it worthily and continue to cultivate it. For this to happen, it is essential to develop "that covenant between human beings and the environment, which should mirror the creative love of God", recognising that we all come from God and that we are all journeying towards him.

General Audience,
26 August 2009

Environment

# Care for the environment

The economic and social costs of using up shared environmental resources must be recognised with transparency and borne by those who incur them, and not by other peoples or future generations. The protection of the environment, and the safeguarding of resources and of the climate, oblige all international leaders to act jointly respecting the law and promoting solidarity with the weakest regions of the world. Together we can build an integral human development beneficial for all peoples, present and future, a development inspired by the values of charity in truth. For this to happen it is essential that the current model of global development be transformed through a greater, and shared, acceptance of responsibility for creation: this is demanded not only by environmental factors, but also by the scandal of hunger and human misery.

General Audience,
26 August 2009

# The Church yesterday, today and tomorrow

In this extraordinary event [of Pentecost] we find the essential and qualifying characteristics of the Church: the Church is *one*, like the community at Pentecost, who were united in prayer and "concordant": "were of one heart and soul".

The Church is *holy*, not by her own merits, but because, animated by the Holy Spirit, she keeps her gaze on Christ, to become conformed to him and to his love.

The Church is *catholic*, because the Gospel is destined for all peoples, and for this, already at the beginning, the Holy Spirit made her speak all languages.

The Church is *apostolic*, because, built upon the foundation of the Apostles, she faithfully keeps their teaching through the uninterrupted chain of episcopal succession.

What is more, the Church by her nature is *missionary*, and from the day of Pentecost the Holy Spirit does not cease to move her along the ways of the world to the ends of the earth and to the end of time.

Regina caeli,
27 May 2007

# With the Holy Spirit

Let us pray that the Lord may bring about
the outpouring of his Spirit now and recreate
his Church and the world. Let us remember
that after the Ascension the Apostles did not
begin as might perhaps have been expected to
organise, to create the Church of the future.
They waited for God to act. They waited for the
Holy Spirit. They understood that the Church
cannot be made, that she is not the product of
our organisation: the Church must be born of
the Holy Spirit. Just as the Lord himself was
conceived and born of the Holy Spirit so the
Church must also be conceived and born of the
Holy Spirit. Only through this creative act of
God can we enter into God's activity, into the
divine action, and cooperate with him... And we
must always implore, over and over again, the
fulfilment of this divine initiative in which we
can become collaborators of God and contribute
to ensuring that his Church is reborn and grows.

Reflection during the First General Congregation
of the Second African Synod,
5 October 2009

# A prayer for forgiveness

[On the cross] The first prayer that Jesus addresses to the Father is a prayer of intercession; he asks for forgiveness for his executioners. By so doing, Jesus is doing in person what he had taught in the Sermon on the Mount when he said: "I say to you that hear, Love your enemies, do good to those who hate you"; and he had also promised to those who are able to forgive: "your reward will be great, and you will be sons of the Most High". Now, from the Cross he not only pardons his executioners but he addresses the Father directly, interceding for them.

Jesus' attitude finds a moving "imitation" in the account of the stoning of St Stephen, the first martyr. Indeed Stephen, now nearing his end, "knelt down and cried with a loud voice, 'Lord, do not hold this sin against them'. And when he had said this, he fell asleep": these were his last words.

General Audience,
15 February 2012

Forgiveness

# God forgives

God forgives all to those who love much. Those who trust in themselves and in their own merits are, as it were, blinded by their ego and their heart is hardened in sin. Those, on the other hand, who recognise that they are weak and sinful entrust themselves to God and obtain from him grace and forgiveness. It is precisely this message that must be transmitted: what counts most is to make people understand that in the Sacrament of Reconciliation, whatever the sin committed, if it is humbly recognised and the person involved turns with trust to the priest-confessor, he or she never fails to experience the soothing joy of God's forgiveness... It is not sin which is at the heart of the sacramental celebration [of reconciliation] but rather God's mercy, which is infinitely greater than any guilt of ours.

Address to the participants in a course on the internal forum organised by the tribunal of the Apostolic Penitentiary, 7 March 2008

# Hope against hope

"Hoping against hope": is this not a magnificent description of a Christian?... We are all members of the peoples that God gave to Abraham as his descendants. Each and every one of us was thought, willed and loved by God. Each and every one of us has a role to play in the plan of God: Father, Son and Holy Spirit. If discouragement overwhelms you, think of the faith of Joseph; if anxiety has its grip on you, think of the hope of Joseph, that descendant of Abraham who hoped against hope; if exasperation or hatred seizes you, think of the love of Joseph, who was the first man to set eyes on the human face of God in the person of the Infant conceived by the Holy Spirit in the womb of the Virgin Mary. Let us praise and thank Christ for having drawn so close to us, and for giving us Joseph as an example and model of love for him.

Mass celebrating the publication of the
*Instrumentum Laboris* of the Second African Synod,
19 March 2009

# Faith, hope and charity go together

"Faith, hope and charity go together. Hope is practised through the virtue of patience, which continues to do good even in the face of apparent failure, and through the virtue of humility, which accepts God's mystery and trusts him even at times of darkness.

Faith tells us that God has given his Son for our sakes and gives us the victorious certainty that it is really true: God is love! It thus transforms our impatience and our doubts into the sure hope that God holds the world in his hands and that... in spite of all darkness, he ultimately triumphs in glory. Faith, which sees the love of God revealed in the pierced heart of Jesus on the Cross, gives rise to love.

Love is the light – and in the end, the only light – that can always illuminate a world grown dim and give us the courage needed to keep living and working. Love is possible, and we are able to practise it because we are created in the image of God.

Pope Benedict XVI, *Deus Caritas Est*, 39

# The musician reflects

In an organ, the many pipes and voices must form a unity. If here or there something becomes blocked, if one pipe is out of tune, this may at first be perceptible only to a trained ear. But if more pipes are out of tune, dissonance ensues and the result is unbearable. Also, the pipes of this organ are exposed to variations of temperature and subject to wear. Now, this is an image of our community in the Church. Just as in an organ an expert hand must constantly bring disharmony back to consonance, so we in the Church, in the variety of our gifts and charisms, always need to find anew, through our communion in faith, harmony in the praise of God and in fraternal love. The more we allow ourselves, through the liturgy, to be transformed in Christ, the more we will be capable of transforming the world, radiating Christ's goodness, his mercy and his love for others.

Blessing of the new organ in Regensburg's *Alte Kapelle*,
13 September 2006

Music

# Music, the language of beauty

I am convinced that music... really is the universal language of beauty which can bring together all people of good will on earth and get them to lift their gaze on high and open themselves to the Absolute Good and Beauty whose ultimate source is God himself.

In looking back over my life, I thank God for placing music beside me, as it were, as a travelling companion that has offered me comfort and joy. I also thank the people who from the very first years of my childhood brought me close to this source of inspiration and serenity.

I thank those who combine music and prayer in harmonious praise of God and his works: they help us glorify the Creator and Redeemer of the world, which is the marvellous work of his hands.

This is my hope: that the greatness and beauty of music will also give you, dear friends, new and continuous inspiration in order to build a world of love, solidarity and peace.

Address following his 80th birthday concert,
16 April 2007

# Bread and Eucharist

Looking closely at this little piece of white Host, this bread of the poor appears to us as a synthesis of creation...

In this way we begin to understand why the Lord chooses this piece of bread to represent him. Creation, with all of its gifts, aspires above and beyond itself to something even greater...

The Lord mentioned its deepest mystery on Palm Sunday, when some Greeks asked to see him. In his answer to this question is the phrase: "Truly, truly, I say to you, unless a grain of wheat falls into the earth and dies, it remains alone; but if it dies, it bears much fruit".

The mystery of the Passion is hidden in the bread made of ground grain. Flour, the ground wheat, presuppose the death and resurrection of the grain. In being ground and baked, it carries in itself once again the same mystery of the Passion. Only through death does resurrection arrive, as does the fruit and new life.

Mass of Corpus Christi,
15 June 2006

# Kneeling before the Blessed Sacrament

We Christians kneel only before God or before the Most Blessed Sacrament because we know and believe that the one true God is present in it, the God who created the world and so loved it that he gave his Only Begotten Son. We prostrate ourselves before a God who... knelt before us to wash our dirty feet. Adoring the Body of Christ, means believing that there, in that piece of Bread, Christ is really there, and gives true sense to life, to the immense universe as to the smallest creature, to the whole of human history as to the most brief existence. Adoration is prayer that prolongs the celebration and Eucharistic communion and in which the soul continues to be nourished: it is nourished with love, truth, peace; it is nourished with hope, because the One before whom we prostrate ourselves does not judge us, does not crush us but liberates and transforms us.

Mass of Corpus Christi,
22 May 2008

# Transforming love

Through the consecrated bread and wine, in which his Body and his Blood are really present, Christ transforms us, conforming us to him: he involves us in his work of redemption, enabling us, through the grace of the Holy Spirit, to live in accordance with his own logic of self-giving, as grains of wheat united to him and in him...

Let us walk with no illusions, with no utopian ideologies, on the highways of the world bearing within us the Body of the Lord, like the Virgin Mary in the mystery of the Visitation. With the humility of knowing that we are merely grains of wheat, let us preserve the firm certainty that the love of God, incarnate in Christ, is stronger than evil, violence and death. We know that God prepares for all men and women new heavens and a new earth, in which peace and justice reign – and in faith we perceive the new world which is our true homeland.

Mass of Corpus Christi,
23 June 2011

# On his resignation

In these last months I have felt my energies declining, and I have asked God insistently in prayer to grant me his light and to help me make the right decision, not for my own good, but for the good of the Church. I have taken this step with full awareness of its gravity and even its novelty, but with profound interior serenity. Loving the Church means also having the courage to make difficult, painful decisions, always looking to the good of the Church and not of oneself...

God guides his Church, he sustains it always, especially at times of difficulty. Let us never lose this vision of faith, which is the one true way of looking at the journey of the Church and of the world. In our hearts, in the heart of each of you, may there always abide the joyful certainty that the Lord is at our side: he does not abandon us, he remains close to us and he surrounds us with his love.

General Audience,
27 February 2013

# The Spiritual Testament

When, at this late hour of my life, I look back on the decades I have wandered through, I see first of all, how much reason I have to give thanks. Above all, I thank God himself, the giver of all good gifts, who has given me life and guided me through all kinds of confusion; who has always picked me up when I began to slip, who has always given me anew the light of his countenance. In retrospect, I see and understand that even the dark and arduous stretches of this path were for my salvation and that he guided me well in those very stretches...

Finally, I humbly ask: pray for me, so that the Lord may admit me to the eternal dwellings, despite all my sins and shortcomings. For all those entrusted to me, my heartfelt prayer goes out day after day.

29 August 2006

# Thoughts on his own death

I can only say that in the slow waning of my physical forces, inwardly I am on a pilgrimage towards Home. It is a great grace for me to be surrounded, on this last part of the road, sometimes a bit tiring, by such love and goodness that I never could have imagined. In this sense, I consider the question of your readers as an accompaniment. I can only thank them and assure you all of my prayers.

*Letter to Corriere della Sera,*
7 February 2018

Peace

" Teach us, Mary, to believe, to hope, to love with you; show us the way that leads to peace, the way to the Kingdom of Jesus. You, Star of Hope, who wait for us anxiously in the everlasting light of the eternal Homeland, shine upon us and guide us through daily events, now and at the hour of our death. Amen!

Act of veneration to the
Immaculate at the Spanish Steps,
8 December 2007

" Jesus Christ did not organise campaigns against poverty, but he proclaimed the Gospel to the poor, providing an integral redemption from moral and material misery.

Angelus,
1 January 2009